PRO SPORTS CHAMPIONSHIPS
TOUR de FRANCE

Grant Gilbert

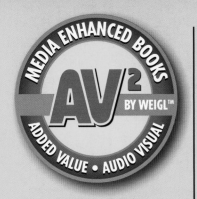

AV² provides enriched content that supplements and complements this book. Weigl's AV² books strive to create inspired learning and engage young minds in a total learning experience.

Your AV² Media Enhanced books come alive with...

Audio
Listen to sections of the book read aloud.

Key Words
Study vocabulary, and complete a matching word activity.

Go to **www.av2books.com**, and enter this book's unique code.

Video
Watch informative video clips.

Quizzes
Test your knowledge.

BOOK CODE

N821700

Embedded Weblinks
Gain additional information for research.

Slide Show
View images and captions, and prepare a presentation.

AV² by Weigl brings you media enhanced books that support active learning.

Try This!
Complete activities and hands-on experiments.

... and much, much more!

Published by AV² by Weigl
350 5th Avenue, 59th Floor
New York, NY 10118

Website: www.av2books.com   www.weigl.com

Library of Congress Cataloging-in-Publication Data
Gilbert, Grant.
Tour de France / Grant Gilbert.
   p. cm. — (Pro sports championships)
Includes index.
   ISBN 978-1-62127-369-1 (hardcover : alk. paper) — ISBN 978-1-62127-374-5 (softcover : alk. paper)
1. Tour de France (Bicycle race)—History—Juvenile literature. I. Title.
GV1049.2.T68G55 2013
796.6'20944—dc23
                              2012043082

Printed in the United States of America in North Mankato, Minnesota
1 2 3 4 5 6 7 8 9 0 17 16 15 14 13

012013
WEP301112

PROJECT COORDINATOR Aaron Carr   EDITOR Steve Macleod   ART DIRECTOR Terry Paulhus

Every reasonable effort has been made to trace ownership and to obtain permission to reprint copyright material. The publishers would be pleased to have any errors or omissions brought to their attention so that they may be corrected in subsequent printings.

Weigl acknowledges Getty Images as the primary image supplier for this book.

CONTENTS

What is the Tour de France?

The Tour de France is one of the world's most popular bicycle races. It takes place in France every July. The best bicycle racers from around the world take part in the event. The riders race across France. Some portions of the race stretch into other countries. In different years, parts of the race have been held in England, Germany, and Spain.

The race is three weeks long. Riders compete every day, except for an occasional rest or travel day. There are two rest days most years.

The Tour de France is one of the most difficult bike races in the world. The race continues in extremely hot weather and when it rains. The course is also challenging. It winds up and down steep mountains, through city streets, and along country roads. Riders must be able to climb steep hills and **sprint** at high speeds. The Tour de France is a test of skill and **endurance**. Finishing the tour is considered a great accomplishment.

Alexandre Vinokourov of Kazakhstan won the 21st **stage** of the 2005 Tour de France. This stage ended on the Champs Elysees on July 24.

CHANGES THROUGHOUT THE YEARS

PAST	PRESENT
Racing bikes were made of heavy steel.	Bikes are made of lightweight materials such as carbon fiber, titanium, and aluminum.
In the first Tour de France, the top 20 racers came from two different countries.	In the 2012 Tour de France, the top 20 racers came from 15 different countries.
The prize for the winner of the first Tour de France was 6,075 Francs.	The prize for the winner of the 2012 Tour de France was 450,000 Euros.
Riders wore little or no safety equipment and regular clothes.	Riders wear helmets, gloves, safety padding, and cycling clothes.

The number of riders competing in the race has varied throughout the years. Riders enter the Tour de France as part of a team. There were 22 teams and 198 riders in 2012. The riders race along a new part of the route, or stage, each day.

The Yellow Jersey

At the end of each stage, the leader of the race is presented with a yellow jersey. The leader is the racer with the fastest overall time. This person wears the yellow jersey for the next stage of the race. This lets fans know which rider is the current leader. Often, the rider who wins a stage is not the overall leader. The yellow jersey was first presented in 1919. The color yellow was chosen because it was the same color as the paper used in the magazine that **sponsored** the Tour de France.

Tour de France History

The first Tour de France race took place in 1903. A magazine owner named Henri Desgrange decided to sponsor a bike race that would travel through France. He wanted the race to challenge the riders. He thought it should take place over several weeks and have a number of stages. The winner of the race would be the rider with the best overall time.

The first race started and ended in Paris. It traveled through many French towns and cities, such as Lyon, Marseille, Toulouse, and Bordeaux. Sixty racers started the first Tour de France. Only 17 riders finished the course. A French cyclist named Maurice Garin won the race. His average speed during the race was 16 miles (25.7 kilometers) per hour.

Tour officials decided to change the course each year. They thought this would keep the race interesting for cycling fans. The direction of the race was changed each year as well. One year it would travel in a clockwise direction. The next year it would move in a counter clockwise direction.

The first mountain stage was added to the race in 1910. That year riders had to race through a section of the Pyrenees. It is a mountain range along the border between France and Spain. The following year, the race traveled through the Alps. These mountains stretch across France, Italy, Austria, and Germany. The Tour continues to pass through these two mountain ranges today.

The highest point in the 1910 race was along Tourmalet. It is one of the highest roads in the Pyrenees with an elevation of 6,939 feet (2,115 meters).

In the early history of the Tour de France, racers sometimes rode on dirt paths to avoid uneven or broken pavement on the roadways.

Parc des Princes stadium in Paris, France, was the finishing point of the 1933 Tour de France.

The original race had six stages and was 1,509 miles (2,428 km). One of the longest Tour de France races was held in 1987. It started in Berlin, Germany, and ended in France. The course had 25 stages. Racers traveled 2,629 miles (4,231 km).

Tour de France Mascot

A racing fan named Didi Senft began acting as the Tour's unofficial mascot in 1993. Senft dresses up like the devil. It is a tribute to his favorite cyclist Claudio Chiappucci, who is nicknamed "El Diablo." Senft holds a pitchfork and has horns. He encourages all the racers. He follows the tour from the beginning to the end. He travels to each of the towns that the Tour passes through. Senft missed the Tour de France in 2012. He was resting at home in Germany after having surgery. Senft is well known for another reason. He built the world's largest bicycle. It is 25.6 feet (7.8 meters) long and 12 feet (3.7 m) high.

Rules of the Ride

The Tour de France has rules the riders must follow. This keeps the competition fair for everyone. Some of these rules are written in a rule book. Others are good sportsmanship. The penalties for breaking these rules can range from a fine to disqualification from the race.

1 Starting the Race

All racers must sign up to enter the race. There are three types of starts in a Tour stage. In a standing start, the race begins where the riders sign-up. In a deferred standing start, the stage begins some distance from the sign-up area because of space restrictions. A rolling start is used if the race begins close to the sign-up area.

2 Motor Vehicles

A rider is not allowed to ride behind a motorbike or car. Racers cannot hang on to the open window of a car. Riders are usually allowed to receive medical attention from the team car while the car is in motion.

3 Numbers

Riders must have an official double-sided number plate attached to their bike frame. Riders must also wear the number on each hip or on the their back, depending on the stage.

4 Substance Testing

Tests are done before and after every race. However, riders can be tested for performance-enhancing substances at any time. Scientists have found certain types of **stimulants** can make a person ride faster. These drugs can be dangerous. They can damage a rider's heart and other organs. Riders who are caught taking them may be **suspended** from racing.

6 Sportsmanship

Riders must respect each other during the race. They should not ride faster if another rider crashes. Riders are expected not to pass the race leader if he is eating, drinking, or on a bathroom break.

5 Helmets

Every rider must wear a helmet. The only time a rider can take off the helmet is during steep mountain climbs.

Making the Call

There are three sets of officials that rule over the Tour de France. One set of officials organizes the start, and records the finishing times. They ensure all riders have signed up for the race and assign them a number. Other officials travel in cars and drive behind the riders during the race. They ensure racers are following the rules. They watch for anything that might give teams or riders an unfair advantage. A third group of officials inspect the riders' equipment. They weigh each bike to ensure that it weighs at least 15 pounds (6.8 kilograms). If a bike is too light, the rider must put small weights on the frame to increase its weight.

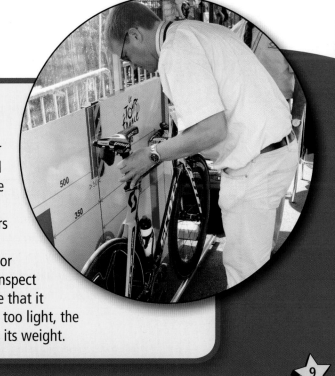

The Tour de France Route

The 2005 Tour is a good example of how the tour route works. The Tour moved clockwise that year. There were 21 stages in the race. It had three mountain finishes, two rest days, 44 miles (74 km) of individual **time trials**, and 40 miles (66 km) of team time trials.

The 2005 Tour began with an 11-mile (19-km) individual time trial sprint. Cyclists raced from the town of Fromentine to Noirmoutier en-L'Île, on the Atlantic coast of France. The tour moved east and had two stops in Germany, at Karlsruhe and Pforzheim. From there, the route turned south to Mulhouse. This part of the course included the first mountain route. The riders had a rest day and flew to Grenoble to continue the race. The route then traveled along the border of Italy and Spain. There was another rest day in the town of Pau. Racers continued through the French countryside until they reached St-Etienne. Then, they took a train to Corbeil Essonnes. This is where the final stage of the race was held. The Tour ended at the Champs-Elysées, which is a famous street in downtown Paris.

Racers must maneuver between cars and other riders to complete the course.

Riders on the Team

Individual riders win the tour, but they require the help of a team. There are nine riders per team. Each rider has different skills. Some riders are strong climbers and other riders are better sprinters. The leader is the rider that the team believes has the best chance to win the race. Riders often travel in small groups called a *peloton*. A team's leader rides in the middle or back of the peloton because there is less wind **resistance**. Having the wind blocked from the leader allows him to save energy for sprinting or climbing up steep hills and mountains. Once the race is underway, the role of leader may go to someone else on the team. A crash or illness can hurt the leader and another rider may take over. Most riders know they will not win the race. Their job is to help their team leader win. The top team at the Tour de France also wins an award.

2013 TOUR de FRANCE ROUTE

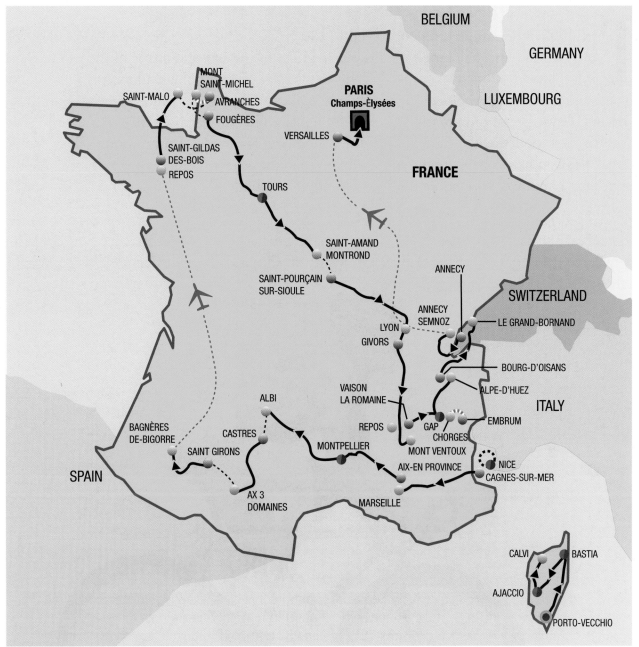

LEGEND

- ● Tour de France start point
- ● Stage start point
- ● Stage end point
- ● Rest point/Stage start point
- ● Stage end/Next stage start
- ■ Tour de France finish point
- ○ Individual time trial
- ✈ Travel by plane
- - - - - Team time trial

Cycling Equipment

The most important equipment a cyclist must have is a bicycle. The bikes used in the Tour de France are custom-made to fit the size and shape of the rider. Most professional cyclists use bikes made of carbon frames. Carbon is solid, but lighter than the steel frames used to make old racing bicycles. The bikes also have special **pneumatic** tires that are lightweight and narrow. They have a thin, smooth **tread**. The wheels of the racing bike are made of aluminum **alloy**. The drop handlebars are positioned lower than the seat or saddle. This puts the rider in a more **aerodynamic** posture. The front and back wheels are closer together than on regular bikes.

Riders wear special cycling shoes. These shoes have a lock on each sole that connects to the pedal. This stops the racers' feet from slipping off the pedals as they ride.

Helmet

Aerodynamic cycling suit

Drop handlebars

Seat/saddle

Carbon bike frame

Cycling shoes

Pedal

Professional cyclists wear racing suits made of sweat-resistant material that is dimpled like a golf ball. The suits are tight-fitting and make the riders more aerodynamic. Racers wear special types of clothing for different weather. If it rains, they have rain gear to keep them dry. If the weather is hot, riders wear a light jersey that keeps them cool. For safety, riders wear helmets. This protects their head from injury.

Riders must hold on to the handlebar for a long period of time. Gloves are worn to prevent blisters and to protect the hands if the rider falls.

Gloves

Sole lock

Jersey Winners

In addition to the yellow jersey, three other racers are honored with a special jersey at the end of the Tour de France. The green jersey is given to the rider who earns the most points during the race. At the end of each stage, points are earned by the riders, depending on their finish in that stage. The red polka dot jersey is awarded to the best climber. Each tour has a number of hills and mountains along the course. Points are given to the riders who reach the top of these hills and mountains the fastest. The white jersey is given to the fastest rider who is 25 years of age or younger on January 1 of the year the tour takes place.

Qualifying to Ride

Teams must be invited to compete in the Tour de France. Invitations are given to the best professional racing teams in the world. Each team is known by the name of its main sponsor.

Usually, between 20 and 22 teams participate in the Tour de France. Teams are chosen based on how they do in other road cycling events held during the year. The *Union Cycliste Internationale* (UCI) is the international governing body of cycling. It awards points to riders based on their performance in the races. These events vary in length. Some events last one day and others can last one week or longer.

Two of the other events are called Grand Tours. They are similar to the Tour de France in length. One takes place in Italy. It is called the Giro d'Italia. The other takes place in Spain. It is known as the *Vuelta a España*. The three major races are known as the "triple crown of cycling."

The Giro d'Italia is a three-week race that takes place in May and June each year. The race was first held in 1909. The leader of this race wears a rose-colored jersey. Ryder Hesjedal from Canada won the 2012 Giro d'Italia.

Cyclists often race in tight groups during the qualifying races held before the Tour de France.

Racers are allowed to wear a jersey other than their team jersey when they are on the winners' podium.

The Vuelta a España has been held every year in Spain since 1935. Like the Tour de France, its route changes each year, and it includes a number of mountain stages. The race most often takes place in September and finishes in the city of Madrid. The leader of this race wears a Jersey de Oro, or a golden jersey. Alberto Contador from Spain won the 2012 Vuelta a España.

Jan Ullrich of Germany won the Tour de France in 1997 and the Vuelta a España in 1999.

Time Trials

In most Tour de France races, there are three events called time trials. The first is called the prologue. It is held before the first stage of the Tour. It is a short race, or sprint, that is usually less than 5 miles (8 km) long. The winner of this race is the first leader of the Tour de France race. Another event is the individual time trial. In this event, riders race against the clock. This race is rarely more than 32.1 miles (50 km) long. The winner is considered to be the fastest racer in the **field**. The third event is a team trial event. Each team rides together and tries to have the fastest time. Every rider on the team must start the race, but only five must finish it. The time of the fifth rider crossing the line determines the team's finishing time.

Where They Ride

When the Tour de France riders see the cobblestone streets of downtown Paris, they know they are close to the finish line of the race.

Most of the stages of the Tour de France are held in France. The starting point changes every year. The race often includes stops in countries near the border of France. In the past, the race has passed through Italy, Spain, Switzerland, Belgium, Luxembourg, Germany, and the Netherlands. The 2012 race began in Liege, Belgium, before heading east and entering northern France.

Until 1975, the race finished at the Parc de Princes stadium in western Paris. Since then, the traditional finish of the Tour has been in Paris on the Champs-Elysées. The entire street is closed down for the end of the race.

Hundreds of journalists cover the Tour de France each year.

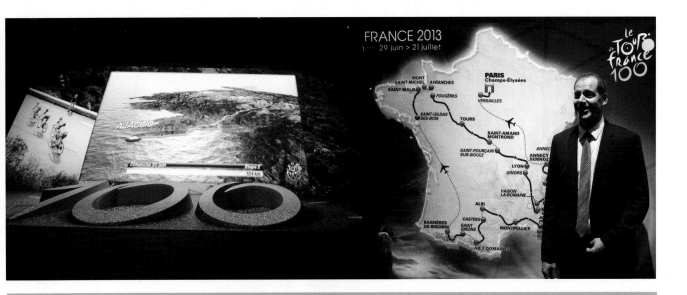

The 2013 Tour will be the 100th edition of the race. It will start on the French island of Corsica. It will be the first time since 2003 every stage will be held in France.

Parts of the race have also been held in Great Britain. In 1998, the race started in Dublin, the biggest city in the Republic of Ireland.

The Tour de France started in London, England, for the first time in 2007. It was the third time that the race had visited England. A stage of the race was held in Plymouth, England, in 1974. In 1998, there were races in the cities of Brighton and Portsmouth. The 2007 race began with a 4.9-mile (7.9-km) prologue stage. The race then went to the town of Canterbury. From there, the racers moved on to Belgium and then to France.

Tour De France Jersey Winners 2006–2012			
YEAR	YELLOW	GREEN	RED POLKA DOT
2012	Bradley Wiggins	Peter Sagan	Thomas Voeckler
2011	Cadel Evans	Mark Cavendish	Samuel Sanchez
2010	Andy Schleck	Alessandro Petacchi	Anthony Charteau
2009	Alberto Contador	Thor Hushovd	Franco Pellizotti
2008	Carlos Sastre	Oscar Freire	Bernard Kohl
2007	Alberto Contador	Tom Boonen	Mauricio Soler
2006	Oscar Pereiro	Robbie McEwen	Michael Rasmussen

Mapping the Tour de France

PACIFIC OCEAN

NORTH AMERICA

ATLANTIC OCEAN

Levi Leipheimer

NORTH AMERICA

SOUTH AMERICA

Juan José Haedo

SOUTH AMERICA

SOUTHERN OCEAN

Racers from around the world compete in the Tour de France. This map shows where some of the best riders were born.

RIDERS IN THE 2012 TOUR DE FRANCE BY CONTINENT

AFRICA: 2

ASIA: 19

AUSTRALIA: 8

EUROPE: 155

NORTH AMERICA: 9

SOUTH AMERICA: 1

N
W · E
S

Scale |———| 621 Miles
0   1,000 Kilometers

ARCTIC
OCEAN

Walter Bénetéau

EUROPE

Yukiya Arashiro

ASIA

EUROPE

ASIA

AFRICA

PACIFIC
OCEAN

INDIAN
OCEAN

Robert Hunter

AFRICA

Cadel Evans

AUSTRALIA

AUSTRALIA

Women and Cycling

Although women do not ride in the Tour de France, there are many racing events that women can take part in. The UCI World Championship and the Tour des Flandres are two of the top road races for women that are held each year.

For many years, the unofficial women's Tour de France was a race called the Grande Boucle. The French term Grande Boucle means "Great Loop" in English. The race traveled around France in the shape of a circle. It had 15 stages and featured the top women riders in the world. The Grande Boucle was canceled in 2003, but returned in a smaller format in 2004. The event was held for the last time in 2009.

In recent years, the UCI Road World Championship has become the top women's bike race. The race was first run in 1927 for men. Women had their own competition in the race beginning in 1958. Elsy Jacobs of Luxembourg was the first winner of the women's competition. The race was not held in 1988 and 1994 when the summer Olympics were held in the same year.

Mirjam Melchers-Van Poppel of Holland was the winner of the Tour des Flandres road race in April 2006.

Women have been racing in the Olympic Games since 1984 in Los Angeles. They compete on a course that travels through the city that is hosting the games. In 2012, 67 women competed in the road race at the Olympic games in London, England. The course was 87 miles (140 km). Marianne Vos of the Netherlands won the gold medal.

The course of the 2004 Olympic women's race passed by several historical landmarks, such as the Parthenon in Athens, Greece.

Alfonsina Strada

The Giro D'Italia is one of the three major road races held in Europe each year. Like the Tour de France, it does not allow women to compete. However, in 1924, a woman did get to compete in the race. Alfonsina Strada registered for the race using the name Alphonse. Organizers thought that she was a man. It was not until the day before the race that they discovered she was a woman. The organizers allowed Strada to ride. She was one of only 30 riders to finish the race. Strada continued to race until the age of 60. Her success made it possible for women racers such as Luisa Tamanini (right) to make a living as a professional bike racer.

Historical Highlights

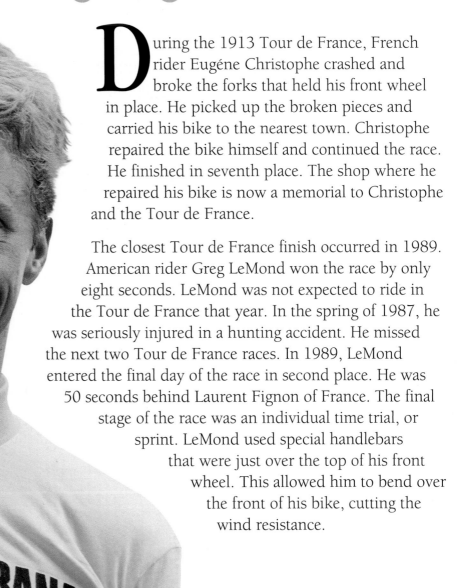

During the 1913 Tour de France, French rider Eugéne Christophe crashed and broke the forks that held his front wheel in place. He picked up the broken pieces and carried his bike to the nearest town. Christophe repaired the bike himself and continued the race. He finished in seventh place. The shop where he repaired his bike is now a memorial to Christophe and the Tour de France.

The closest Tour de France finish occurred in 1989. American rider Greg LeMond won the race by only eight seconds. LeMond was not expected to ride in the Tour de France that year. In the spring of 1987, he was seriously injured in a hunting accident. He missed the next two Tour de France races. In 1989, LeMond entered the final day of the race in second place. He was 50 seconds behind Laurent Fignon of France. The final stage of the race was an individual time trial, or sprint. LeMond used special handlebars that were just over the top of his front wheel. This allowed him to bend over the front of his bike, cutting the wind resistance.

Greg LeMond was the first North American racer to win the Tour de France three times.

LeMond had one of the fastest time trials in the history of Tour de France and won the race. It was the last time a sprint stage has ended the Tour race.

In 1997, Jan Ullrich of Germany won the Tour de France by more than nine minutes. It was one of the largest margins of victory in the history of the Tour. Ullrich was only 23 years of age.

The last rider from France to win the Tour was Bernard Hinault. He won the race for the fifth time in 1985.

TOUR DE FRANCE RECORD HOLDERS

TOUR RECORD	RECORD HOLDER	COUNTRY
Most Tour Appearances – 17	George Hincapie	United States
Most Yellow Jersey Wins – 5	Jacques Anquetil	France
	Bernard Hinault	France
	Miguel Indurain	Spain
	Eddy Merckx	Belgium
Most Green Jersey Wins – 6	Erik Zabel	Germany
Most Red Polka Dot Jersey Wins – 7	Richard Virenque	France
Most Days in Leader's Jersey – 111	Eddy Merckx	Belgium
Youngest Tour Winner – 19 years old	Henri Cornet	France
Oldest Tour Winner – 36 years old	Firmin Lambot	Belgium

LEGENDS
and Current Stars

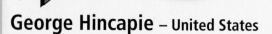
George Hincapie

Robbie McEwen – Australia

Robbie McEwen was born in 1972. He began racing at a young age. McEwen started racing BMX bikes. This is a type of bike used on dirt courses. He became the Australian National Champion. When McEwen turned 18, he began road racing. He was good at sprinting. McEwen could accelerate quickly, which often helps a rider win a race.

In 1994 and 1995, McEwen was on the Australian National Road Team. During that time, he won 50 races. McEwen then decided to turn professional. He was named Australian Cyclist of the Year in 2002 and 2005. His first Tour de France was in 1997. He finished in 117th place.

McEwen has competed in the Tour de France 12 times. He has won the green jersey three times.

George Hincapie – United States

George Hincapie was born in 1973 in New York City. He started racing as a teenager and won the Junior World Road Cycling Championships in 1990. Hincapie has ridden in the Tour de France 17 times.

In 1998, Hincapie became the United States' National Road Race Champion. He won the event again in 2006 and 2009.

Hincapie has competed in five Olympic Games. He competed for the U.S. in the 1992, 1996, 2000, 2004, and 2008. Hincapie is one of the tallest riders, at 6 feet 3 inches (193 cm), in the history of the Tour de France.

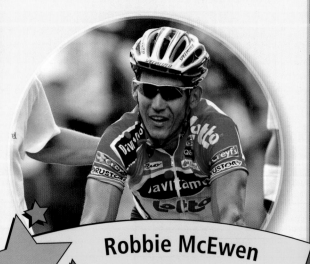
Robbie McEwen

Alberto Contador

Alberto Contador – Spain

Alberto Contador was born in 1982. He began racing competitively at 15 for a local cycling team. In 2002, Contador won the Spanish National Time-Trial Championship in the Under-23 division. He turned professional the next year and won his first race at the Tour of Poland.

Contador won the Tour de France in 2007 and in 2009. In 2008, he won the other two Grand Tour events, the Giro d'Italia and the Vuelta a España. He was only the fifth rider ever to win cycling's Triple Crown by winning all three Grand Tour events.

Mark Cavendish – Great Britain

Mark Cavendish trained as a cyclist in the British Olympic Academy program. He was a Commonwealth Games champion. His first full season as a professional was in 2007. He won the points jersey in five major races that year.

Between 2008 and 2010, Cavendish won 15 stages at the Tour de France. He won the green jersey at the Tour de France in 2011. Also during 2011, he won the rainbow jersey as the winner of the World Championships.

Cavendish competed at the 2012 Olympics in London, England, and won a gold medal for Great Britain.

Mark Cavendish

Famous Firsts

François Faber of Luxembourg was the first rider to win five consecutive stages of the Tour. He did this during the 1909 race. Faber was the first racer born outside of France to win the tour.

In 1910, the Tour organizers wanted to add some excitement to the race. They asked the riders to race up a mountain pass in the Pyrenees. The route was muddy and covered in snow. Race officials worried the riders would not be able to complete the route. However, most of the racers made it up and down the steep mountain. This started the tradition of including the Pyrenees mountain stages in the Tour de France.

Jacques Anquetil wore the yellow jersey in every stage of the 1961 Tour de France.

During the 1906 race, the route passed through the city of Metz. At the time, Metz was part of Germany. This marked the first time the race route traveled outside of France.

French racer Jacques Anquetil was the first cyclist to win the Tour de France five times. He won his first race in 1957. He then won the event four times in a row from 1961 to 1964.

Midway through the 1919 Tour de France, race organizers decided to give a special jersey to the race leader. When the Tour reached the city of Grenoble, a yellow jersey was given to the race leader, Eugène Christophe. He was the first Tour de France racer to wear the yellow jersey.

René Pottier of France was the winner of the first Tour de France race to have a stage in Germany.

During the 1999 Tour de France, Italian racer Mario Cipollini became the first rider to win three stages in a row since Gino Bartali in 1948.

Vicente Treuba of Spain was the first rider to be called "King of the Mountains." In 1933, race organizers decided to give a special red polka dot jersey to the top racer in the mountain stages of the Tour. Treuba was the first rider to win the best climber jersey.

Mario Cipollini of Italy won 12 stages of the Tour de France during his 14-year career as a professional racer.

American Road Racing

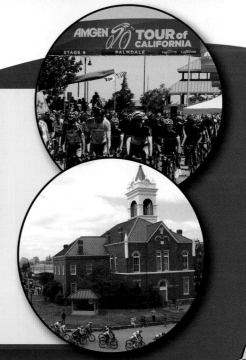

There are two major road races held in the United States each year. The Tour of California and the Tour of Georgia. The Tour of California was started in 2006. The race is 700 miles (1,127 km). It lasts eight days and is held in February. In 2007, the race had seven stages. It started in San Francisco and finished in Long Beach, near Los Angeles. Eighteen teams took part in the race. The Tour of Georgia began in 2003. It attracted large crowds, proving there was great interest in the sport of road cycling in the United States. The race is held over six days and covers more than 600 miles (966 km).

The Rise of the Tour de France

1903

The first Tour de France race is held. Sixty riders compete in the event. Racers ride during the night to complete the course.

1910

The first mountain stage is introduced. Stage nine of the race goes through the Pyrenees. Octave Lapize wins the stage and the Tour de France.

1919

The yellow jersey is given to the race leader for the first time.

1922

Firmin Lambot (left) becomes the first Tour winner not to win a single stage.

1926

One of the longest Tour de France races is held. It is 3,570 miles (5,745 km) long.

1930

Teams are organized by country for the first time. André Leducq of France wins the race. Teammate Charles Pélissier wins a record eight stages.

1940–1947

The Tour is suspended for eight years because of **World War II**.

1962

Sponsors form their own teams for the first time since 1929.

1969

Belgium racer Eddy Merckx wins the yellow, green, and red polka dot jerseys.

1985

Bernard Hinault of France wins the Tour de France for the fifth time.

1986

Greg LeMond becomes the first American to win the race.

2012

Bradley Wiggins becomes the first cyclist from Great Britain to win the Tour de France.

QUICK FACTS

- Only 10 of 69 riders finished the race in 1919.

- The riders in the Tour will collectively go through 42,000 bottles of water in the course of the Tour. The empty bottles are highly valued by fans as souvenirs.

Test Your Knowledge

1 When was the first Tour held?

2 What color jersey does the Tour leader wear?

3 Who was the first American to win the race?

4 Why does the tour's unofficial mascot dress up in a devil costume?

5 What piece of safety equipment must every rider wear?

6 How long was the race in 1926?

7 What are three triple crown cycling races?

8 What Tour de France record belongs to George Hincapie?

9 When did women start competing in cycling at the Olympics?

10 In which city does the race always finish?

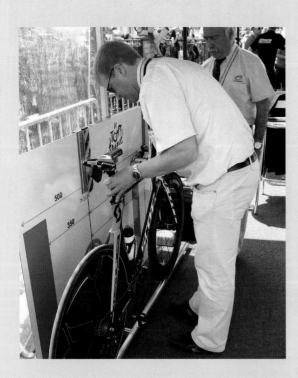

Answers: 1) 1903 2) Yellow 3) Greg LeMond 4) It is a tribute to his favorite rider Claudio Chiappucci. He was nicknamed "El Diablo." 5) A helmet 6) 3,570 miles (5,745 km) 7) The Tour de France, the Giro d'Italia, and the Vuelta a España. 8) Most appearances with 17. 9) In Los Angeles in 1984. 10) Paris

Key Words

aerodynamic: having a shape that reduces the drag or resistance of air across it

alloy: a metal made by mixing two or more metals

endurance: the ability of something to last or to withstand wear and tear

field: all the participants in a contest or sport

pneumatic: containing air or gas pressure

resistance: the slowing or stopping of something

sponsored: provided funds for a project or activity

sprint: a short, fast race in cycling

stage: the Tour route over one day, from start to finish

stimulants: substances that increase activity

suspended: temporarily prevented from continuing or being in force

time trials: parts of a race where the quickest time is declared the winner

tread: the part of a bike that grips the road

World War II: a war that lasted from 1939 to 1945 and included the continents of Asia, Africa, Australia, Europe, North America, and South America

Index

Log on to www.av2books.com

AV² by Weigl brings you media enhanced books that support active learning. Go to www.av2books.com, and enter the special code found on page 2 of this book. You will gain access to enriched and enhanced content that supplements and complements this book. Content includes video, audio, weblinks, quizzes, a slide show, and activities.

AV² Online Navigation

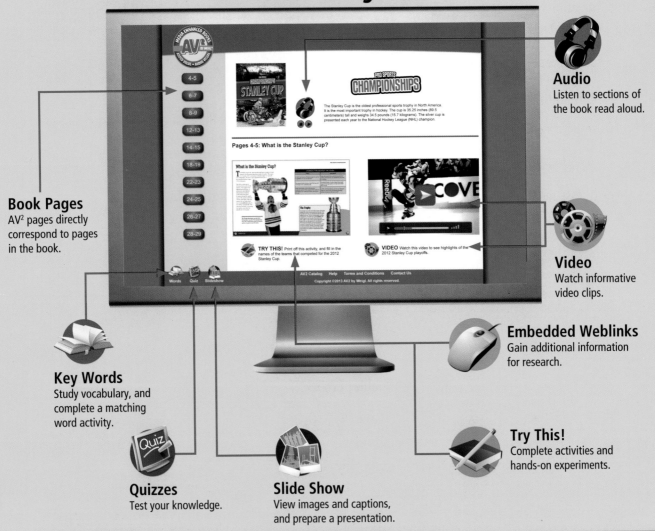

Audio
Listen to sections of the book read aloud.

Book Pages
AV² pages directly correspond to pages in the book.

Video
Watch informative video clips.

Embedded Weblinks
Gain additional information for research.

Key Words
Study vocabulary, and complete a matching word activity.

Try This!
Complete activities and hands-on experiments.

Quizzes
Test your knowledge.

Slide Show
View images and captions, and prepare a presentation.

AV² was built to bridge the gap between print and digital. We encourage you to tell us what you like and what you want to see in the future.

Sign up to be an AV² Ambassador at
www.av2books.com/ambassador.